Scotland's Glory

by
Patrick Laughlin

Contents

Jarrold Publishing, Norwich

Introduction

To define Scotland's glory is to attempt the impossible. No other country of similar size summons up such powerful and passionate images of landscape, history and culture, and few nations inspire such depth of feeling amongst their people as does Scotland.

To many, Scotland's glory is its scenery. Here, from some of the oldest rocks known to man, nature carved out what many consider to be the most beautiful landscape on earth – the Scottish Highlands. Other countries might have higher peaks, deeper lakes and broader valleys, but the unique Scottish combination of mountain, loch and glen continues to capture the hearts of all who witness it.

To some, Scotland's glory is its history. Despite invasions by Romans, Vikings and English, Scotland has never been wholly conquered, and has always fiercely defended at least a measure of independence. The legacy of centuries of external bloodshed and internal warfare is the continued existence, in these more peaceful times, of countless castles and battle-fields, and poignant memories of such romantic figures as Robert Bruce, Mary Queen of Scots and Prince Charles Edward Stuart.

To others, Scotland's glory is its people. Scots are proud of their country without being fanatical; they are enterprising and inventive – as all those who watch television, listen to radio, or ride bicycles along tarred roads will attest; they are creative in the fields of literature, art and music; and, above all, they are renowned for their friendliness and hospitality.

To still others, Scotland's glory is its culture; not just the traditional embodiments of Scottishness like haggis, heather and bagpipes – potent though these symbols may be – but a living, dynamic culture which has made its influence felt throughout the world. Who has not savoured Scotch whisky, swung a golf club, or sported something tartan?

Perhaps Scotland's glory lies in its sheer variety. Variety of climate, certainly – it is said, with some truth, that in Scotland one can encounter all four seasons in a single day. Variety of language, with Gaelic still widely spoken in the Highlands and Islands; variety of accent, too, with Scots from different areas speaking both the purest and (to some) most unintelligible forms of the English language imaginable. Or variety of lifestyle, with the noise and bustle of the Lowland cities being worlds away from the tranquillity of a Highland croft.

Indefinable, then, though Scotland's glory might be, a brief journey through these pages will capture at least some of the essence of this remarkable nation.

Elgol, on the Isle of Skye, is dominated by the Cuillin Hills

The Borders

The Scottish Borders are the first sight and taste of Scotland for visitors from around the world, and yet all too many are content to pass quickly through this enchanting area, over-anxious to reach the more familiar delights of Edinburgh and the Highlands beyond.

All is peaceful in this land of rolling hills and fertile farmlands, and it is difficult to believe that for centuries this was perhaps the most fought-over territory on earth. But those prepared to pause awhile and explore the Borders will discover an astonishingly rich historical legacy, together with a friendly people who, despite their geographical proximity to England, are fiercely proud to be Scottish.

The turbulent history of the Borders can best be told through its buildings, and most famous of all are the four magnificent abbeys of Jedburgh, Melrose, Kelso and Dryburgh. All four abbeys were founded in the twelfth century by David I, and all were destroyed and rebuilt several times during the centuries of English invasion and Scottish resistance, before finally falling into ruin after the Reformation. Despite this common past, each of the Border abbeys has its own charm: Jedburgh, the best preserved, which stands proudly on a hillside, surrounded by its historic town; Melrose, beneath whose soaring arches Robert Bruce's heart is buried; Kelso, the wealthiest – and hence the most ransacked – of the abbeys; and beautiful, honey-stoned Dryburgh, romantically situated on the River Tweed.

Whilst the abbeys were not built to withstand the continual attacks and skirmishes of the Border wars, numerous castles and fortified homes stand today as reminders of a bygone violent age. Amongst them are lovely Traquair House, visited by no fewer than twenty-seven monarchs, fourteenth-century Hermitage Castle, a grim fortress with a bloody history, and thick-walled Neidpath Castle, once besieged by Cromwell, which lies near the popular resort of Peebles. However, it would be unfair to lay all of the blame for the Borders' stormy past at the feet of the English. Much of the warring and lawlessness came from the so-called 'Border reivers' – the cattle raiders whose bitter family feuds often lasted for generations. Today, the great rivalries between Border towns are fought out on the rugby field, for this is the heartland of Scottish rugby.

Many Border communities relive their rich histories each year through the unique spectacles of the common ridings. These colourful ceremonies, watched by huge crowds, generally involve mass ride-outs by townsmen inspecting the burgh boundaries on horseback. Particularly moving is Selkirk's 'casting of the colours', which commemorates the return in 1513 of the sole local survivor of Flodden's tragic battlefield.

With such a tradition to draw on, it is little wonder that Scotland's foremost historical novelist and antiquarian, Sir Walter Scott, chose to live in the Borders. He created a home for himself, named it Abbotsford in remembrance of local monks, and filled it with Scottish treasures; it is now one of the most-visited attractions in the country. Abbotsford is by no means, however, the grandest house in the Borders. As more peaceful times descended following the Unions between Scotland and England, great country mansions were built by wealthy landowners. Floors Castle, close to the pretty town of Kelso, is a vast architectural extravaganza; nearby lies Mellerstain House, a perfect essay in Georgian design by William and Robert Adam. Bowhill, near Selkirk, has a richly-furnished interior, whilst Manderston is an Edwardian house with the world's only silver staircase.

The wool industry has long been a vital component of the Borders economy, and several towns are renowned for their high-quality tweeds and woollen goods. Though weaving had been carried out for centuries previously, it was during the Industrial Revolution that centres like Hawick and Galashiels boomed. The characteristic two-coloured patterns of tweed were first created in Jedburgh, and have since become famous throughout the world. The story of the industry – as well as its products – can be discovered at several mills and museums on the Borders Woollen Trail.

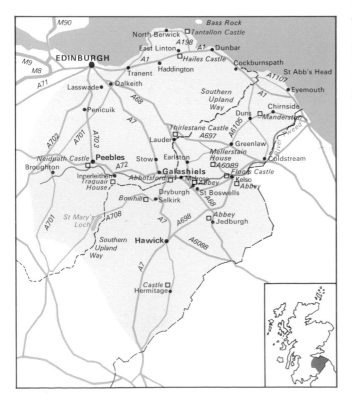

A completely different facet to the Borders is revealed along the Berwickshire coastline. Here, fishing and smuggling, rather than farming and marauding, were the traditional ways of life. Eyemouth still has a busy commercial harbour, and the spectacular stacks and cliffs around St Abbs Head are populated by countless thousands of teeming seabirds.

Further up the coast, the superb beaches of East Lothian are seemingly lined by a series of fine links golf courses, with Muirfield taking pride of place. The holiday and golfing resorts of Dunbar and North Berwick benefit from the highest sunshine records in Scotland, while dramatic Tantallon Castle looks out over the Firth of Forth to the distinctive Bass Rock. Inland, East Lothian's lush farmlands are dotted with delightful red pantiled villages, and the Georgian market town of Haddington is particularly attractive.

There could be no better introduction to the glories of Scotland than the Borders.

Well-preserved Jedburgh Abbey dates from the twelfth century

Dryburgh Abbey enjoys a peaceful location

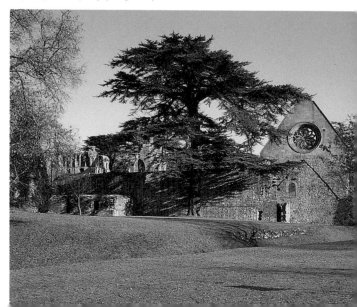

Traquair House is one of Scotland's most historic homes

During Selkirk's Common Riding, the Royal Burgh Standard Bearer 'casts the colours'

Abbotsford, Sir Walter Scott's home, sits on the banks of the Tweed

*Scott's View to the Eildon
Hills is the best-loved
panorama in the Borders*

*Floors Castle is the most grandiose
of the Borders' historic houses*

*The Museum and Scott Art
Gallery in Hawick*

*The woollen mills of the Borders are
eagerly sought out by bargain hunters*

*A typically elegant Scottish bank
house, Haddington*

Tantallon Castle looks o
to the Bass Roc

Edinburgh

Edinburgh, Scotland's capital, is one of the most written-about and photographed cities on earth. Its dramatic skyline, all-pervading sense of history and cultural sophistication make an indelible impression on every visitor.

Edinburgh is a delight to explore on foot; most of its attractions are contained within a compact central area split clearly between the Old Town and the New Town, and a plethora of readily-identifiable landmarks make navigation easy. Looming over the city, Edinburgh Castle is the natural starting-point for any visit. There has been a castle on this great volcanic rock since the Dark Ages, with today's castle being a collection of buildings ranging from the tiny eleventh-century Queen Margaret's Chapel, through medieval apartments containing the Scottish Crown Jewels, to more modern barracks (still fully utilised). From the castle ramparts there are stupendous views over Edinburgh to the Lothians, Fife and the Highlands beyond.

Leaving the castle via the Esplanade, which houses the spectacular Edinburgh Military Tattoo each August, one of Europe's most historic streets beckons – the Royal Mile. In fact, the Royal Mile is four streets (Castlehill, Lawnmarket, High Street and Canongate) linked end-to-end; this was the spinal cord of Edinburgh's Old Town, and history seeps from its every stone. Lined with tall densely-packed tenements, the cobbled street acted as meeting-place and market-place, as a place of public festivities and public executions. Along its length today are dozens of attractions, too numerous to mention, but, for all its museums, churches and craft centres, the Royal Mile is still very much a working, living street. At its foot, beneath the brooding Salisbury Crags and Arthur's Seat, lies the Palace of Holyroodhouse, official Scottish residence of the monarchy. The palace, particularly renowned for its Mary Queen of Scots associations, is a splendid example of Renaissance architecture.

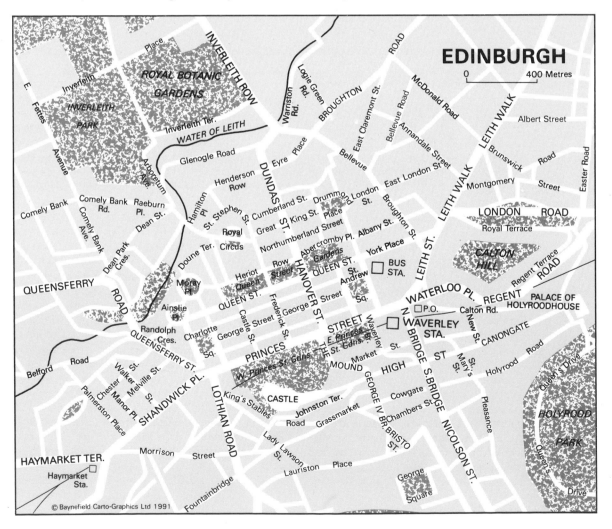

Princes Street Gardens, overlooked by Edinburgh Castle, are a haven of peace in the city centre

However, Edinburgh's principal architectural glories date from the Georgian period. In the eighteenth century, the wealthy inhabitants of the overcrowded Old Town, tired of their noisy and insanitary living conditions, created for themselves a new town of wide avenues, elegant squares and sweeping crescents. The New Town became a byword for gracious living, and nowadays it is financiers, accountants and architects who discreetly inhabit most of the rooms behind the neo-classical façades.

The aestheticism of the New Town was reflected in Edinburgh's growing cultural status. Literature, art and philosophy blossomed during the period known as the Scottish Enlightenment, when the city was home to romantic writers like Scott and Burns, gifted artists such as Wilkie and Raeburn, and eminent philosophers like Hume and Smith. Edinburgh gained the soubriquet of 'Athens of the North', no doubt helped by its many memorials and statues, with the grouping of monuments on Calton Hill and the towering Scott Monument on Princes Street being especially notable.

The legacy of the Scottish Enlightenment has enabled Edinburgh to retain its position as an international centre of culture. The city is home to the National Galleries of Scotland, with separate collections of general art, portraits, modern art and antiquities. In addition, there are many smaller galleries displaying traditional and modern works, and scores of museums and historic buildings open to visitors. The highlight of the cultural year, however, is the Edinburgh International Festival. Held each August since 1947, the Edinburgh Festival, in conjunction with its associated Fringe, has become the largest arts festival in the world. For three weeks, the city takes on a carnival air. Every possible public space, from 3,000-seat theatre to school playground, from concert hall to church hall, is utilised, with performers and audiences alike sharing in the delights of drama, opera, street entertainments and music of every description.

These are but a few of the better-known facets of the jewel that is Edinburgh. It is a city crammed with unexpected delights: the vista over the Firth of Forth which suddenly opens up from a dark Old Town close; the sentimental statue of the faithful terrier, Greyfriars Bobby; the richly ornate Victorian pub interiors; the specialist shops in streets off the main tourist thoroughfares; the luxuriant palms in the beautifully-maintained Royal Botanic Gardens. As Edinburgh grew in size, it swallowed up once-outlying settlements, but several of these maintain their own individual character. The peaceful Dean Village lies half-hidden along the tree-lined Water of Leith; Stockbridge is Edinburgh's bohemian quarter; and pleasure boats berth at the pretty village of Cramond.

Leith, Edinburgh's port, retains an independent spirit, and, though its waterfront is increasingly crammed with restaurants and luxury apartments, it is still a down-to-earth, hard-working community. Slightly further afield are the magnificent Adam mansion of Hopetoun House, the ruins of Linlithgow Palace and lesser-known treasures, such as Roslin Chapel.

But it is always difficult to bid farewell to Scotland's capital, for Edinburgh is, quite simply, one of the world's great cities.

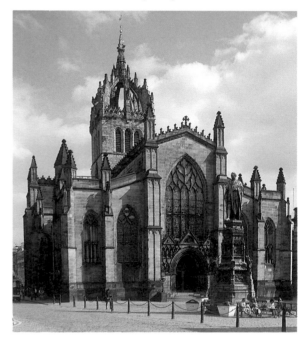

*The incomparable spectacle of
Edinburgh Military Tattoo*

*John Knox's House on the historic
Royal Mile*

*St Giles Cathedral is Edinburgh's
principal church*

The splendid Palace of Holyroodhouse is a landmark in Scotland's capital city

The gracious architecture of Edinburgh's New Town is seen at its best in Charlotte Square

Edinburgh's skyline – a riot of spires, towers and crags

Princes Street is one of Europe's finest thoroughfares

The port of Leith has become a fashionable meeting-place

Festival time in the city

Fife

Most visitors will enter Fife by crossing one of the Forth bridges, and there could be no finer introduction to this unique corner of Scotland. Together, standing side by side, the graceful suspension road bridge and the massively-cantilevered rail bridge form one of the country's great spectacles; and, as the traveller reaches the northern shore of the Firth of Forth, there is a real sensation of having arrived in an identifiably separate region. Fife is different. It was known in former times as the Kingdom of Fife, and its inhabitants have always delighted in its independent character – an independence which reveals itself today in Fife's distinctive countryside, buildings and local accent.

Two of the lesser-known glories of Fife lie to the west of the Forth bridges. Culross is a little town which was a thriving trading port in the sixteenth and seventeenth centuries; though its importance declined, its buildings survived and have been restored to provide a marvellously authentic glimpse into Scottish domestic life prior to the Industrial Revolution. The much larger town of Dunfermline, once capital of Scotland, has at its centre the twelfth-century abbey in which are interred Robert Bruce's remains.

The coastal road travelling east passes through small resorts like Aberdour and Kinghorn, best known for their beaches, then through the industrial towns of Kirkcaldy and Methil, before entering Fife's most picturesque district – the East Neuk. The word 'neuk' means 'corner', and this is the easternmost corner of Fife, jutting out into the North Sea. Its half-dozen or so fishing villages are famous for their charm and unspoiled character, with their whitewashed cottages, red pantiled roofs and colourful harbours.

The East Neuk ports were at their most prosperous in medieval times, when they traded with countries throughout Europe. The crow-stepped gables on many older buildings, influenced by Flemish architecture, are the most visible evidence of these past continental links. When European trading declined, fishing became the staple industry, and, though the herring fleets which packed the harbours of Anstruther and St Monans are no more, smaller-scale fishing continues to the present day. Pittenweem is now the principal fishing port, with shellfish and crustaceans the local speciality.

Inland, Fife's patchwork countryside is criss-crossed by a network of roads which wind through pretty villages. Ceres, with its green and folk museum, and Falkland, dominated by its palace, are particularly memorable. Sixteenth-century Falkland Palace, fortified yet superbly ornate, was built by James IV and V as a country residence for the Stuart kings and queens. The royal visitors, including Mary Queen of Scots, hunted deer and boar in the local forests, and played royal or 'real' tennis on the palace's court. But it was in more tragic circumstances that Mary returned to this area in 1567. She was imprisoned for eleven months in the island castle on Loch Leven, just to the east, and, though rowed to freedom, she was soon reincarcerated by Elizabeth I, and was never to return to Scotland.

One of Queen Mary's pursuits in happier times was the game of golf, and, in Fife, all roads eventually seem to lead to the home of golf, St Andrews. Early records show that golf was played here as early as 1547; two centuries later, The Society of St Andrews Golfers was formed by local gentlemen. This Society was to become the Royal and Ancient Golf Club, now the international headquarters of the sport. The 'R and A' clubhouse, built in 1854, looks out on to the first tee and eighteenth green of the most famous golf course in the world, the Old Course. Golf, a way of life throughout Scotland, is more of an obsession in Fife, and, as well as the five renowned courses – and the British Golf Museum – in St Andrews, there are many other fine courses in the area.

However, long before golfers strode its links, St Andrews was attracting visitors. This was the centre of Scotland's Christian faith, and as such a place of pilgrimage. Legend has it that St Rule was shipwrecked here in the eighth century. He was carrying with him relics of St Andrew, and enshrined them in a church which became St Andrews Cathedral – the largest cathedral in Scotland, now a magnificent ruin. The twelfth-century castle nearby was originally the bishop's palace, but later gained notoriety as the scene of some bloody incidents during the Reformation; its infamous Bottle Dungeon can still be seen. St Andrews University, dating from 1411, is Scotland's oldest, and today's students keep alive many of its traditions.

St Andrews, with its fine beaches, is now a popular resort, but few other holiday destinations can offer such an entrancing mix of old and new. A stay in this historic town makes a fitting climax to any visit to Fife.

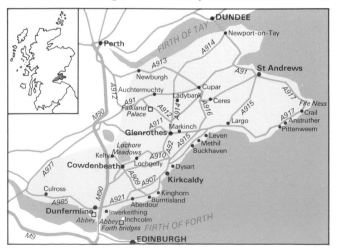

The magnificent Forth Bridge is one of the world's most recognisable structures

Culross is a beautifully-preserved seventeenth-century village on the River Forth

Twelfth-century Dunfermline Abbey overlooks Pittencrieff Park

Crail has the East Neuk of Fife's most picturesque harbour

Dysart's whitewashed and crowstepped cottages are typical of the Fife coast

Falkland Palace was the country residence of Stuart monarchs

Loch Leven Castle, where Mary Queen of Scots was imprisoned in 1567

The Royal and Ancient Clubhouse overlooks the famous Old Course at St Andrews

St Andrews Castle houses the notorious Bottle Dungeon

St Rule's Tower forms part of the extensive remains of St Andrews Cathedral

The Central Highlands

The Central Highlands is Scotland's heartland, both geographically and historically. Here, where the Highlands and the Lowlands meet, is a region of dazzling scenic contrasts. To the south and east lie fertile agricultural lands and rolling hills, while to the north and west rise the mountains, dissected by deep lochs and narrow glens.

This area has been described as the Scottish Lake District, and with good reason. Lochs large and small are scattered throughout, with the best known being Loch Lomond. This beautiful stretch of water, whose 'bonnie banks' have been immortalised in song, still acts as a magnet for countless visitors. In summer, pleasure craft scud around the loch's many islands, and picnickers throng its shoreline, overlooked by walkers enjoying the panoramic views from Ben Lomond.

Several of the other lochs in the vicinity are similarly guarded by high mountains. The distinctive pyramidical shape of Schiehallion looms over lonely Loch Rannoch; Ben Lawers' massive bulk dominates steep-sided Loch Tay; water-sports enthusiasts on Loch Earn are overlooked by Ben Vorlich; and the ascent of Ben Venue is rewarded by the sight of Loch Katrine glistening below.

Rivers as well as lochs play an important part in the life of the Central Highlands. The River Tay – Scotland's longest at 119 miles (192 km) – flows the length and breadth of Perthshire. Stretches of the Tay are amongst the world's most prized angling waters; each January, a parade of fishermen through Kenmore's picturesque square celebrates the opening of the salmon season. Further south, the river flows serenely past Dunkeld's historic cathedral. Dunkeld is a gem of a village; its lovingly-restored 'little houses'

were built when the original settlement was burned down following the Battle of Killiecrankie in 1689.

The Tay has witnessed many of Scotland's most historical moments. Birnam Hill, one of many steep wooded slopes flanking the river, is immortalised in Shakespeare's *Macbeth*. Macbeth was one of the forty-two Scottish kings crowned at the abbey of Scone, further downstream. Scone's coronations took place atop the mystical Stone of Destiny, until it was stolen in 1296 by Edward I and taken to Westminster Abbey. Scone Abbey was totally destroyed during the Reformation, but the story of its kings is related nearby at stately Scone Palace.

More historical associations are evident in the 'Fair City' of Perth, whose fine Georgian buildings and green parklands border the wide River Tay. Perth was at one time Scotland's capital and, despite its inland situation, it prospered as a trading centre, thanks largely to the navigable river. To the present day, the Tay and its tributaries are central to the city's economy, draining its rich agricultural hinterland (renowned for soft fruits, in particular Blairgowrie raspberries) and providing the clean, fresh water for Perth's famous whiskies.

The River Forth rises amongst the densely-wooded hills of the Trossachs – particularly beautiful in their autumn colours. Here is a district beloved of artists, poets and writers, with Sir Walter Scott foremost amongst them. Scott's imagination was fired by the Trossachs; many of his romantic works were inspired by its striking landscapes. His most famous Trossachs character, Rob Roy Macgregor, was no legendary figure, but a real Highland adventurer – variously described as a cattle thief and a proud clan leader – whose daring exploits continue to enthral.

The Forth flows close by the holiday centres of Aberfoyle and Callander before meandering across its wide floodplain to the historic town of Stirling. Like Edinburgh's Old Town, Stirling shelters beneath a mighty castle atop a volcanic rock. Its strategic location made it a fortress settlement from earliest times, with Stirling Castle eventually becoming the seat of the Stuart royal court. The towering Wallace Monument commemorates the victor of the Battle of Stirling Bridge in 1297. Seventeen years later, Robert Bruce vanquished the English army at nearby Bannockburn; a heritage centre now recalls this, the most famous victory in Scotland's battle-scarred history.

As the Forth widens, it passes beneath the dramatic escarpment of the Ochil Hills, from which tumble the tributaries that powered the textile looms of the 'Hillfoot' towns. The textile industry, though no longer dependent on water power, has survived, and a Mill Trail is a popular attraction. In fact, crafts are a particular feature of the Central Highlands. Seemingly

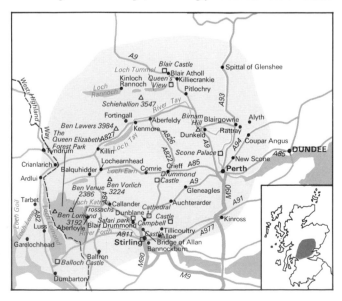

Ben Lomond looms over the waters of Loch Lomond

Perthshire's Queen's View is one of Scotland's best-known panoramas

The Braes of Balquhidder – Rob Roy country

around every corner there are glassblowers, horn carvers, potters, leatherworkers and many other craftspeople inviting visitors to their home workshops.

Visitors have traditionally been made welcome in this part of the world. Resorts like Crieff, Aberfeldy and Pitlochry have been looking after travellers between the Highlands and Lowlands for centuries, and modern-day visitors can also choose from an almost inexhaustible fund of places to visit. Superb historic monuments like Blair Castle and Dunblane Cathedral complement modern attractions such as Perth's Leisure Pool and Pitlochry Festival Theatre; with the bonus of the marvellous surrounding scenery, few would dispute that the Central Highlands contains all that is good about Scotland.

Pleasure cruising beneath the wooded crags of Loch Katrine

The broad River Tay is renowned for its salmon angling

The attractive small town of Dunkeld was completely rebuilt following the Battle of Killiecrankie

The River Tay flows eastward beneath Kinnoull Hill, close to Perth

Stirling Castle, perched high on a crag

The Trossachs, seen at their best near Aberfoyle

Robert Bruce gazes over Bannockburn

Handloom weaving at the Scottish Tartans Museum in Comrie

The pretty Perthshire village of Fortingall has a 3,000-year-old yew tree

Blair Castle is one of the most-visited historic locations in Scotlan

The North-East

With over eighty castles, more than half of the world's malt whisky distilleries, dramatic mountain and coastal scenery, and activities ranging from skiing to salmon angling, the north-east is almost more Scottish than Scotland itself.

Dundee, with its superb setting on the Firth of Tay, is the gateway to the north-east. This 'city of three js' (jute, jam and journalism) has diversified its industries in recent years, and has Scott's Antarctic exploration ship RRS *Discovery* as the centrepiece of its revitalised waterfront. Just up the Angus coast – which has several fine beaches – lies Arbroath, whose now-ruined abbey was the scene of the signing of the Scottish Declaration of Independence in 1320. Arbroath smokies (haddock smoked over wood chips) are a renowned delicacy. Inland, the turrets of Glamis Castle rise above soft-fruit fields in the broad valley of Strathmore. Glamis, reputed to be Scotland's most haunted castle, has been a royal residence since 1372.

But it is to Deeside, across the Grampian mountains, that the epithet 'royal' is most often attached. For here, in the forests beneath dark Lochnagar, is Balmoral Castle, holiday retreat of the Royal Family since its surroundings first captured the heart of Queen Victoria. In nearby Braemar, the Highland Gathering, held on the first Saturday of September, attracts huge crowds, as eager to watch members of the Royal Family as they are to enjoy the spectacle of piping, dancing and caber-tossing.

The Rivers Dee and Don flow eastward through wooded countryside which is particularly beautiful in

autumn. Nowhere else in Scotland can boast such a profusion of castles, each different from the last. Drum Castle has a stout thirteenth-century tower, and the glorious gardens at Crathes Castle are amongst the best in Britain. Beautiful Craigievar Castle has a fairytale aspect, while, back on the coast, Dunnottar Castle, perched dramatically atop high cliffs, is guarded on three sides by the often-ferocious North Sea.

Scotland's third-largest city, Aberdeen, owes much to the North Sea. For centuries a fishing and trading port, Aberdeen became the oil capital of Europe in the 1970s, and its large harbour owes much of its continuing prosperity to the marine traffic which supplies and services the offshore oil rigs. Aberdeen is a handsome city; its granite buildings, sparkling in the sunlight, are complemented by marvellous floral displays in parks, gardens and alongside main roads, with roses blooming in abundance during the summer months. Leafy Old Aberdeen, with its cathedral and crown-spired King's College, is a haven of peace in this bustling city.

Still more castles lie to the north and west, amongst some of Scotland's best agricultural land, with Haddo House (famed for its choral society), the splendidly-refurbished Fyvie Castle and the Georgian baroque of Duff House worthy of special note. The attractive town of Elgin has an evocative ruined cathedral, while the twentieth-century monks at nearby Pluscarden have rebuilt their 700-year-old abbey. Sturdy fishing towns and whitewashed villages are strung out all round the north-east coast. The largest of these harbours, Peterhead, is in fact the largest whitefish port in Europe, and an early-morning visit to its fish market, where the vigorous Buchan dialect can be heard at its broadest, is an experience to savour.

Some of the country's best freshwater angling is to be found on the River Spey, but the pure soft waters of Speyside have an even more famous by-product – whisky. Dozens of distilleries, some with internationally-known names and others almost unknown to the outside world, nestle in the north-east countryside. Each produces a single malt whisky with its own individual bouquet and flavour, as visitors who follow the Malt Whisky Trail can discover for themselves. Despite many attempts, no other country has succeeded in replicating the unique characteristics of Scotch whisky; its apparently simple ingredients of water and malted barley acquire an elusive magic when distilled over peat fires and left to mature for many years in wooden casks.

The fast-flowing Spey rises high in the heart of the Grampians, and along its valley, in the shinty-playing district known as Badenoch, lie several small towns. Kingussie's Highland Folk Museum gives an insight into the bygone ways of life of the Highland peoples, while the Landmark Centre at Carrbridge is a modern

Dundee is superbly sited on the Firth of Tay

Ruined Arbroath Abbey, signing-place of the Scottish Declaration of Independence

attraction which interprets the natural history of the area in an educational yet entertaining fashion. The best-known resort is Aviemore, which is busy throughout the year thanks to the proximity of the ski slopes at Cairngorm – one of the north-east's three winter sports areas. The Cairngorm mountains are the highest mountain group in Britain, with three peaks over 4,000 ft (1,219 m); in their shadow, ospreys fly over Loch Garten, and brightly-coloured dinghies on Loch Morlich contrast vividly with the dark surrounding forests.

The north-east cannot fail to make a memorable impact on all those who discover its charms.

*Golden daffodils surround Glamis
Castle in springtime*

*Scotland's most famous royal
residence is Balmoral Castle
on Deeside*

The gardens at Crathes Castle are amongst the best in the country

Tossing the caber – the traditional highlight of Braemar's Highland Gathering

The fairytale turrets of Craigievar Castle, near Alford

Aberdeen's fine floral displays complement its granite buildings

Dunnottar Castle has a spectacular site near Stonehaven

Fettercairn Distillery has a traditional pagoda-style roof

The Forest Tower at Carrbridge's Landmark Centre

Cairngorm is a popular destination for Scottish skiers

The tiny harbour at Pennan is sheltered beneath high cliffs

The Northern Highlands

The Northern Highlands is a region of unforgettable colours. Here, amidst some of Europe's most spectacular and unspoiled scenery, the traveller will experience turquoise seas, silver sands, purple heathers and orange sunsets, their hues brought even more vividly to life by the clean, sparkling air.

Inverness, the capital of the Highlands, is a thriving centre which greets visitors with the saying *ceud mile fàilte* – a hundred thousand welcomes. Highlanders are naturally courteous and kind to all their guests, but one unwelcome visitor in 1746 was the Duke of Cumberland, whose army finally vanquished the ill-fated Jacobites, led by Prince Charles Edward Stuart, at nearby Culloden. The battlefield today is a melancholy, windswept moor, preserved for posterity by the National Trust for Scotland.

To the south-west of Inverness lies long narrow Loch Ness, legendary home of the famous monster. The first recorded sighting of Nessie was in the sixth century, but despite scientific expeditions, underwater exploration and millions of tourist photographs, the monster has resisted all attempts to prove – or disprove – her existence. Urquhart Castle is a popular vantage-point for Nessie-watchers, while Drumnadrochit's Loch Ness

Monster Exhibition tells the full mysterious tale.

The coastal journey northwards provides little indication of the dramatic landscapes to be found further west. The charming little spa town of Strathpeffer, the fertile fields of the Black Isle and Dornoch's championship golf course are all set in gentle scenery, with wooded hills, sandy beaches and wide seascapes aplenty. Tiny fishing villages dot the coastline before the two towns of Caithness, Wick and Thurso, are reached. Wick has a busy fishing harbour, and Thurso was an important centre for trade between Scotland and Scandinavia in the Middle Ages. However, it was not a Scandinavian but a Dutchman who gave his name to the best-known settlement in Caithness. Jan de Groot's fifteenth-century ferry service to Orkney is long gone, but his name lives on at John o' Groats, at the tip of the British mainland (though the most northerly point is actually Dunnet Head, to the west).

The great summits of Ben Loyal and Ben Hope loom over the wild, lonely flow country of Caithness. It is a strangely mournful wilderness of peat bogs and lochans, rich in flora and bird life. The human history of the area is equally sad, for it was Caithness and Sutherland which were worst affected by the infamous Highland Clearances of the nineteenth century. The Northern Highlands were seen as ideal for wool production, and landowners, often using brutal methods, forced families off their crofts to make way for sheep. Thousands became destitute, failing to scrape a living from fishing, and starvation was widespread. Eventually most of the people either moved to the southern cities or emigrated to North America. Reminders of this unhappy period cannot be avoided; ruined townships and crofts can still be seen in every glen.

The far north-west of Scotland has a landscape unlike any other in Britain. The coastline is magnificent, with high sandstone cliffs, deserted beaches and dozens of tiny islands, but it is the imposing mountains which are most memorable. Standing in isolated splendour, peaks like Canisp, Stac Polly and the sugar-loaf Suilven dominate the scene, providing a stunning backdrop to Lochinver's harbour and overshadowing other natural glories, like Britain's highest waterfall, Eas Coul Aulin.

The fishing port of Ullapool stands on Loch Broom, one of the many sea-lochs which serrate the rugged coast of Wester Ross. Ullapool, like the nearby resort of Gairloch, is the base for pleasure cruisers which cater for birdwatchers, anglers and sightseers. However, it is an inland stretch of water, Loch Maree, which has been called the most lovely of Highland lochs; overlooked by the steep-sided Slioch, its wooded shores are wildly beautiful. Close by is the famed Inverewe Garden, a

Inverness Castle overlooks the River Ness

showpiece of sub-tropical horticulture, where exotic plants and shrubs flourish in an often-balmy environment created by the warming Gulf Stream.

Further south, the scenery becomes, if anything, even more grandiose. The massive mountains of Torridon – Beinn Eighe, Liathach and Beinn Alligin – present a challenge to the most experienced of walkers and climbers, and the prospect of seeing rare species like the pinemarten and golden eagle is an added attraction. In fact, the Beinn Eighe National Nature Reserve was the first area in Britain to be so designated. To the south, on the shores of Loch Carron, lies the picturesque village of Plockton, whose palm trees and whitewashed cottages provide a Riviera-like ambience. Trains on the stunning Kyle Line run through Plockton en route to the terminus at Kyle of Lochalsh, the ferry port for Skye. Loch Alsh itself links with Loch Duich, where, in the shadow of the majestic Five Sisters of Kintail, the picture-postcard Eilean Donan Castle stands guard on its rocky islet.

Amidst such magnificence, it is hard to disagree with those who assert that the Northern Highlands is the most beautiful place on earth.

The memorial cairn at Culloden

Urquhart Castle sits above
Loch Ness

Majestic Suilven towers over
Loch Assynt

The harbour at John O'Groats

Ullapool is an important west coast fishing port

Sub-tropical plants flourish at Inverewe Garden

Sunset at Diabaig on Loch Torridon

The village of Plockton is idyllically situated on Loch Carron

The Five Sisters of Kintail rise above Glen Shiel and Loch Duich

Eilean Donan Castle – quintessentially Scottish

Highland cattle at Torridon

Smoo Cave, on Sutherland's northern coast

The Islands

Scots have always had a special affinity with the sea; however, for Scottish islanders past and present, the relationship has been more akin to dependence. The sea provides sustenance, transport and employment, and the islanders respect its awesome power and beauty.

The Northern Isles, Orkney and Shetland, are often grouped together by politicians, mapmakers and weather forecasters, but to do so is to ignore their distinctive personalities. The Orkney Isles, perhaps surprisingly, are low-lying, green and fertile, which made them a natural target for successive waves of invaders: first Stone Age peoples, then Picts and finally Vikings. Throughout Orkney there are scores of archaeological sites, with the three best-known being on the largest island, Mainland. Skara Brae is a 4,000-year-old village whose dwelling-houses, furnishings and implements were preserved under sand until excavation; Maes Howe is a massive Stone Age burial cairn; and the Ring of Brodgar is a well-preserved stone circle. Orkney's capital, Kirkwall, is dominated by the twelfth-century St Magnus Cathedral, while, for those in search of other spiritual comfort, Scotland's most northerly whisky distillery lies nearby.

Shetland, too, has some outstanding prehistoric remains, but the Viking influence is much stronger than in Orkney. The local dialect has a distinctively Nordic character, as do many placenames, and Shetlanders relate with pride that their nearest railway station is in Bergen, Norway. To celebrate these Scandinavian links, the Up Helly Aa fire festival, highlighted by the burning

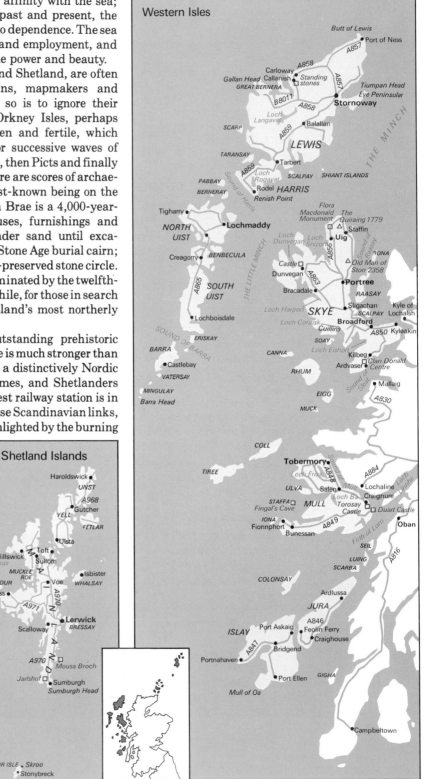

The 4,000-year-old settlement of Skara Brae on Orkney is a mecca for archaeologists

of a longboat, is held each January in the capital town of Lerwick. The long winter nights are traditionally the time for knitting the distinctively-patterned woollens for which Shetland and nearby Fair Isle are famed, while, in contrast, twilight conditions can be enjoyed throughout the night in midsummer. Shetland's skies and spectacular sea-cliffs seem continually alive with gulls, fulmars, puffins and many rarer bird species.

The Western Isles – or, to give them their proper name, the Outer Hebrides – are a world apart from the rest of Scotland. Throughout this long chain of islands, from Lewis in the north to the tiny isles south of Barra, deserted white beaches delight the eye, peat smoke gently assails the nose, and the ear is soothed by the lilting Gaelic tongue – for here, uniquely, Gaelic is the first language of the majority of people. Lewis is the most populated of the Western Isles, but even here there is only one town – Stornoway – and many inhabitants live and work on crofts, the traditional small farms. Despite its apparent isolation, Lewis has been settled for thousands of years, with the most dramatic evidence for this being the awesome Standing Stones of Callanish, erected some 4,000 years ago. Ferry services and causeways link many of the Western Isles, but mountainous Harris needs neither, as it is actually part of the same island as Lewis; nevertheless, its separate identity is proudly maintained. The smaller islands to the south, such as North and South Uist, Benbecula and Barra, are renowned for their superb beaches and green, flower-strewn meadows. Interestingly, the islanders south of Benbecula are overwhelmingly Roman Catholic, whilst strict Presbyterianism prevails further north.

The Inner Hebrides, beloved of yachtsmen, are dominated by the Isle of Skye, to which the adjective 'magical' is often applied, and with good reason. Volumes have been written about this most romantic of islands, but no words could fully describe the brooding majesty of the Cuillins, the country's most spectacular mountain range. The Cuillins inevitably dominate Skye, but the island has many other facets, including the dramatic rock formations of the Quiraing and the Old Man of Storr, the principal town of Portree, and the popular attractions of Dunvegan Castle and the Clan Donald Centre. It was from Skye that the fugitive Bonnie Prince Charlie finally escaped his Hanoverian pursuers, bidding farewell to the brave Flora Macdonald.

Further south, beyond the strangely-named 'Small Isles' of Canna, Rhum, Eigg and Muck, lies Mull, a large and hilly island. Divers in Tobermory harbour, overlooked by gaily-coloured cottages, still search for the treasure alleged to be contained in the wreck of a Spanish galleon sunk here in 1588. To the west of Mull are the low-lying islands of Coll and Tiree (which has Britain's best sunshine figures), and the natural wonder of Fingal's Cave on Staffa, which inspired Mendelssohn's *Hebridean Overture*. But most special of all the Inner Hebrides is Iona, a beautiful and gentle island. Here, in AD 563, St Columba established his missionary church, and the island has been a centre for Christianity ever since. The thirteenth-century Benedictine abbey has been carefully restored, and the graves of many Scottish, Norse and Irish kings can be seen. Further south still are the islands of Colonsay, Jura and Islay. The pungent iodine and peat aromas of Islay's malt whiskies make them immediately identifiable, and in many ways they sum up the character of all the islands – recognisably Scottish, but with a distinctiveness which is all their own.

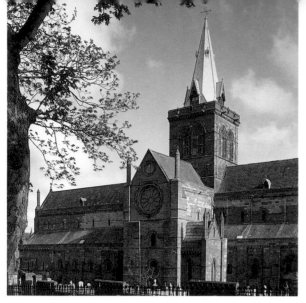

St Magnus Cathedral dominates Kirkwall

The colourful puffin is a common island sight

Shetland's Mousa Broch is particularly well preserved

Up Helly Aa – Lerwick's Viking fire festival

The mysterious Standing Stones of Callanish can be found on the west coast of Lewis

The unspoiled beaches and wide seascapes of Harris are typical of the Outer Hebrides

The Cuillins on Skye are seen at their best in winter

Tobermory is 'capital' of the Isle of Mull

The abbey on the holy island of Iona

Fingal's Cave on Staffa inspired the composer Mendelssohn

The West Coast

The west coast of Scotland is generally recognised as one of the world's finest seaboards. Along its length, deep and narrow sea-lochs penetrate the mountains inland, providing some glorious scenic contrasts, with colourful fishing ports and bustling resorts adding a human dimension to the grandeur of the landscape.

No single location could completely sum up the west coast's romantic appeal, but Glenfinnan must come close to doing so. Here, against the backdrop of the hills around Loch Shiel, stands the Glenfinnan Monument, a lonely column commemorating the occasion in 1745 when Prince Charles Edward Stuart's standard was raised above crowds of cheering clansmen, effectively marking the beginning of the second – and doomed – Jacobite Rebellion. The most spectacular view of the monument can be obtained from the imposing railway viaduct which carries the West Highland Line from Fort William to Mallaig – a route famed for its beauty.

Ben Nevis, Britain's highest peak at 4,408 ft (1,344 m), towers over Fort William. The mountain's northern slopes have in recent times been developed as a winter sports area. Skiing is also enjoyed at Glencoe, to the south; however, this most powerful of Scottish glens has an all-pervasive atmosphere of gloom, doubtless due in part to the infamous Massacre of Glencoe in 1692, when the Campbells, staying as guests of the Macdonalds, slew their sleeping hosts.

One is never far from the coast in Argyllshire, where sailing and angling are popular pursuits; indeed, local seafood is so highly regarded that much of the catch is exported daily to Europe's top restaurants. Oban is Argyll's principal town, and its semi-circular bay, watched over by the colosseum-like folly of McCaig's Tower, is perhaps the most-photographed seafront in Scotland. Oban has been dubbed 'Gateway to the Islands' because of its regular ferry services to the Inner Hebrides. Just inland is Loch Awe, where Kilchurn Castle sits picturesquely beneath Ben Cruachan, a mountain which has been hollowed out to house a hydro-electric power station. Back on the coast, the landscape becomes gentler as the visitor travels southwards. One curiosity is the island of Seil, linked to the mainland by a little stone bridge known – correctly, if a little misleadingly – as the 'Bridge over the Atlantic'.

Kintyre is the name given to the long, narrow peninsula which is so noticeable on any map of Scotland. The pleasure cruisers which glide gently along the Crinan Canal (at the peninsula's northern end) certainly shorten their journeys, but they also miss the charms of one of the country's least-discovered areas. Kintyre's attractions – its sandy beaches, wooded valleys and nectar-like Campbeltown whisky – are understated but abundant.

Loch Fyne, famed for its kippers, probes deeply into the south-western Highlands. Along its shores can be found the gorgeous Crarae Woodland Garden and the charming little town of Inveraray. This is a planned Georgian settlement, built in the second half of the eighteenth century by the 3rd Duke of Argyll to replace an original village. On that site, the Duke created the sturdy Inveraray Castle, which today boasts fine collections of furniture, paintings and porcelain. Close by is Inveraray Jail, a carefully-restored courthouse, where lifelike tableaux portray scenes from the past.

Most visitors to Loch Fyne will travel over the road known as 'Rest and Be Thankful', but, spectacular as the views from this former military routeway are, they give only a hint of the beauties of the Cowal peninsula to the south. At every turn of the roads through the Argyll Forest Park and above the Kyles of Bute, different panoramas of sea, hills and islands open up, with the

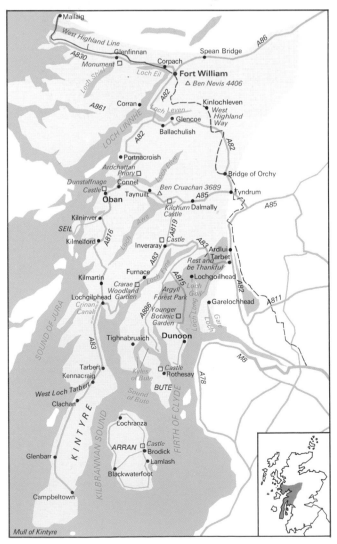

shrubs and trees of the Younger Botanic Garden a particular delight. Dunoon is the main resort, and the highlight of its year comes each August with the huge massed parade of pipe bands which forms part of the Cowal Highland Gathering. Rothesay, on the nearby Isle of Bute, is another of the popular holiday towns on the Firth of Clyde. Its castle, dating from the eleventh century, is one of the most historic in the land, and has associations with such names as Robert Bruce and Oliver Cromwell; the heir to the British throne still holds the title of Duke of Rothesay.

Arran is the major island on the Clyde, and it is packed with interest. Often known as 'Scotland in Miniature', Arran has mountains, glens and sandy beaches, a rich concentration of Bronze and Iron Age relics, and a notable castle at Brodick, the island's capital. It was while sheltering in a cave near the village of Blackwaterfoot that Robert Bruce is said to have watched the famous spider that encouraged him to 'try, try and try again' to unshackle his country from English domination.

This, then, is the west coast. No visit to Scotland would be complete without a sample of its magic.

The incomparable surroundings of the Glenfinnan Monument

The magnificent viaduct at Glenfinnan is crossed by a West Highland steam train

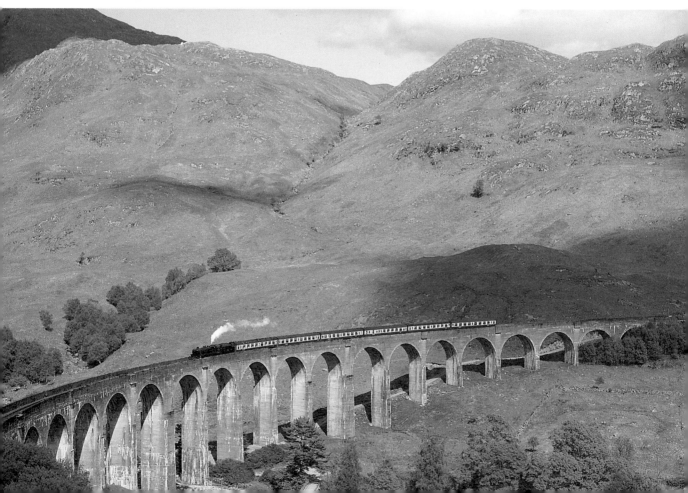

Ben Nevis from Inverlochy

Glencoe's brooding peaks are frequently shrouded by mist

Morar's famous silver sands lie close by Mallaig

Oban is the west coast's main port

Kilchurn Castle guards the eastern end of Loch Awe

Lochranza, on the Isle of Arran

Inveraray Castle, the home of the Dukes of Argyll

Glasgow

When, in the sixth century, the missionary St Mungo founded a monastery church close to the shallow River Clyde, he could not have imagined that a great city would one day grow up on this site known as *Glas Cau*, the green place. St Mungo was obviously not a native Glaswegian; if he were, he would confidently have predicted the seemingly impossible – and then proceeded to make it happen.

To relate the story of Glasgow is to take a rollercoaster ride through economic history, for the city has lurched through centuries of repeated boom and depression. The tiny ecclesiastical settlement in time became a small town, built around the thirteenth-century Gothic cathedral which had replaced St Mungo's original church. The town grew gradually, with an emergent middle class of merchants and traders, but did not really blossom until after the Parliamentary Union of Scotland and England in 1707, when vast new markets were opened up to Scottish importers and exporters. Glaswegian merchants – the so-called 'tobacco lords' – prospered on transatlantic trade in tobacco, sugar and rum, and helped shape a new Glasgow by building mansions and warehouses in an area now called the Merchant City. Today, many of the buildings in these streets have been transformed into luxury apartments, exclusive shops and restaurants.

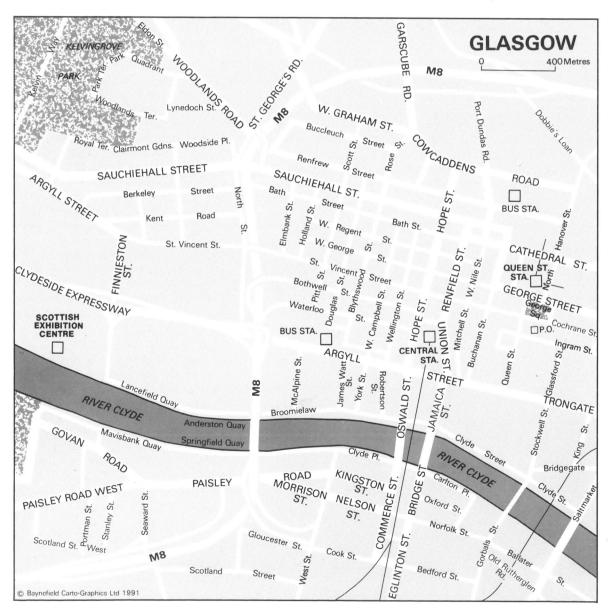

© Baynefield Carto-Graphics Ltd 1991

George Square lies at the heart of Glasgow

However, the American Wars of Independence put an end to the trading boom, and nineteenth-century Glasgow had to find other sources of income. It did so with a vengeance by becoming the 'second city of the Empire' – the heavy engineering capital of the world. The River Clyde became an industrial waterway, transporting iron ore and coal from Lanarkshire as well as finished goods like railway locomotives, and powering the cotton mills which were the country's first large-scale factories. At New Lanark, south of Glasgow, the pioneering mill-owner Robert Owen built a model community (now designated a World Heritage Site) which greatly improved the living and working conditions of textile workers; and there were further innovations in Paisley, where the ever-popular swirled-loop fabric patterns were created.

When the cotton industry declined, the rapidly-expanding city next turned to shipbuilding as its major industry. Clyde-built vessels like the great liners *Queen Mary* and *Queen Elizabeth* spread the fame of Glasgow worldwide before, sadly, most of the shipyards along the river were forced to close. Glasgow is no longer a city of heavy industry, but its magnificent Victorian buildings are a reminder of an age of prosperity. Particularly notable are the extravagant interiors of the City Chambers, which reflect the wealth and confidence of the Victorian age; the flamboyant Templeton's Carpet Factory, inspired by the Doge's Palace in Venice; and, from a slightly later period, the Art Nouveau stylings of the Glasgow School of Art, designed to the last detail by the great architect Charles Rennie Mackintosh.

In recent years, Glasgow has gained a formidable reputation as a city of culture. The creation of a magnificent building to house the famous Burrell Collection did more than provide a long-awaited home for the superb collection of *objets d'art* which had been given to the city; it also helped to focus attention on Glasgow's already rich stock of cultural glories. In the Kelvingrove Art Gallery, the city has Britain's best civic art collection; it has the much-admired People's Palace, a museum celebrating local working-class history; it boasts several famous theatres; and it is home to the highly-rated Scottish National Orchestra, Scottish Opera and Scottish Ballet. Glasgow's contemporary painters and musicians have received international acclaim, and it is a tribute to the city's cultural vitality that many of these artists continue to live and work locally.

But ornate buildings and fine galleries count for nothing without a population to inhabit them, and Glasgow's chief asset has always been its people. Gregarious and garrulous, witty and warm-hearted, Glaswegians have insulated themselves against economic uncertainties by developing an ability to laugh in times of hardship and share in times of plenty. From the wise-cracking bus driver to the cheeky winger on the football field, Glasgow is full of extroverted characters, and though the humour can be rough-edged at times, its earthiness is part of its charm. Another Glaswegian virtue is lack of pretension, and, whether in a fashionable store or at The Barras market, in an East End bar or a West End concert hall, the same down-to-earth attitude prevails. Glasgow possesses a unique blend of egalitarianism and infectious *joie de vivre*.

The motto of Scotland's largest city is 'Let Glasgow Flourish'. It is a statement of intent rather than an expression of hope, and rarely has a motto been better chosen. Glasgow's abiding spirit of enterprise, allied with an unshakeable self-belief, will ensure that the city continues to prosper, ever ready to adapt to changing circumstances whilst retaining its principal feature – its warm heart.

Tugs on the River Clyde

The model industrial village of New Lanark
lies to the south of Glasgow

The ornate Templeton's Carpet Factory

Haggis – Scotland's national dish

*Modern sculpture at the Burrell
Collection*

Glasgow City Chambers

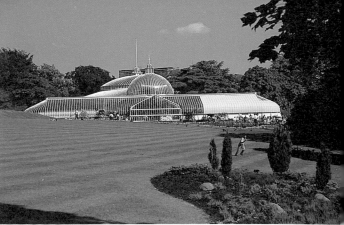

Exclusive shopping at Princes Square

Kibble Palace in the Botanic Gardens

The South-West

The south-west is probably Scotland's most undiscovered region. Its gentle landscapes and calm seascapes are a world away from the traditional rugged picture of Scotland, yet the south-west remains proudly and identifiably Scottish. Here, after all, is the home of Robert Burns, the nation's bard; here is the birthplace of Christianity in Scotland; and here is that most romantic of Scottish locations, Gretna Green.

The Ayrshire coast is one of Scotland's favourite holiday domains, with a string of small resorts like Largs, Troon and Girvan looking westwards over the sea to the Isle of Arran and Ailsa Craig. Ayrshire is another of those Scottish areas which brings a mistiness to the eye of the dedicated golfer, and its championship links at Turnberry, Troon and Prestwick are internationally renowned. Also on this coast is the sumptuous Culzean Castle, a Robert Adam masterpiece which, together with its surrounding country park, is the National Trust for Scotland's most-visited property.

But it is with Robert Burns that Ayrshire is most readily associated. Seemingly every community has a Burns connection, and, travelling through the area, it is not difficult to identify the pastoral scenes and couthie Ayrshire character which inspired the eighteenth-century poet. Burns was born in Alloway, just south of Ayr, and his cottage birthplace has been preserved as a museum. Both in Alloway and in the bustling resort of Ayr itself, there are monuments, museums and memorabilia galore to this most remarkable of Scotsmen – a self-confessed drunkard and womaniser, whose sometimes poignant, sometimes uproarious and always human verse continues to delight and move the world.

Turnberry – one of Scotland's finest golf courses

Burns lived the last few years of his tragically short life not in Ayrshire, but further south in the pleasant market burgh of Dumfries – another town whose museums and hostelries are seemingly crammed with Burnsiana. Dumfries is known as the 'Queen of the South' – a romantic name which belies a history of invasions and feuds as bloody as in any of the Border towns. Just south of Dumfries, on either side of the River Nith, are two of Scotland's finest historic buildings. Caerlaverock Castle is a superb triangular-shaped sandstone fortress, complete with moat, where sixty men withstood a siege by the 3,000-strong army of Edward I in 1300. More moving is the ruined Sweetheart Abbey, a Cistercian monastery founded in the late thirteenth century by Devorgilla Balliol in memory of her husband, John, and so named because she took his embalmed heart to her own grave.

Away from pretty coastal villages like New Abbey and Kippford, the Dumfriesshire hills rise to over 2,500 ft (762 m). Small towns like Langholm and Moffat drew their prosperity from sheep and cattle trading; the remarkable Devil's Beef Tub is a deep, naturally-formed hollow in the hills which was used as a hideout by cattle rustlers. Nearby, the Grey Mare's Tail waterfall plunges spectacularly down a grassy defile.

However, the south-west's chief scenic delights lie further westward, in the beautiful forests, lochs and glens of the Galloway Hills. Though unmistakably Scottish in character, this landscape is somehow more peaceful and unruffled than the wilder Scottish Highlands. The Galloway Forest Park, with its way-marked walks, red deer and wild goats, has at its centre the splendid Glen Trool, where Bruce's Stone marks an early battle victory over the English by Robert Bruce.

Much of Galloway's charm lies in its unspoiled towns and villages, and, in attractive centres like Castle

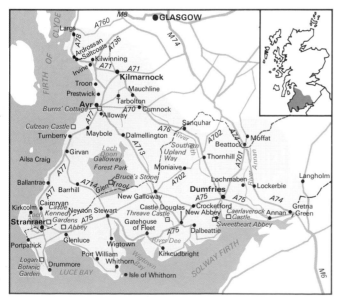

Douglas, Kirkcudbright and Gatehouse of Fleet, the relaxed pace of life is reminiscent of a bygone, less hurried age. The area enjoys Scotland's mildest climate, which, together with the benign influence of the Gulf Stream, is largely responsible for the beauty of some of the country's most colourful gardens. Amongst these gems are Threave, Castle Kennedy and the sub-tropical palms of Logan Botanic Garden.

This last-named garden truly lies in Scotland's south-west, on the peninsula known as the Rhinns of Galloway. Fine coastal scenery stretches down to Scotland's most southerly point, the Mull of Galloway, with the picturesque harbour at Portpatrick looking across the Irish Sea. Modern-day ferries sail from Ireland to Stranraer and Cairnryan, but a much earlier visitor from Ireland was St Ninian, who founded Scotland's first Christian church at Whithorn at the end of the fourth century. Ongoing archaeological excavations continue to uncover more evidence of Scotland's early Christian heritage.

But it is further to the east, close to the English border, that this brief tour of Scotland must end. For countless newly-weds over the centuries, however, Gretna Green's Old Blacksmith's Shop, with its marriage anvil, has symbolised the beginning – not just of Scotland, but of new lives together. It is fitting that so many visits to Scotland begin and end at such a romantic location – for, above all, it is romance, in all its many shapes and forms, that is truly Scotland's glory.

Culzean Castle in Ayrshire is one of Robert Adam's masterpieces

The humble cottage birthplace of Robert Burns at Alloway, near Ayr

The imposing ruins of Caerlaverock Castle

Dumfries stands on the River Nith

The cascades of the Grey Mare's Tail

Bruce's Stone overlooks picturesque Glen Trool

Threave Gardens near Castle Douglas

A red deer stag in the forests of the south-west

Fishing boats and pleasure craft in Portpatrick's harbour look westward across the Irish Sea

The Old Blacksmith's Shop at Gretna Green, the romantic setting for thousands of weddings